Unhindered

STUDY GUIDE

. Lord help me to get through today
↳ daily bread
tomorrow will take care of itself

Cover design by: Joe DeLeon

ISBN: 978-1-950718-75-7   1 2 3 4 5 6 7 8 9 10

Printed in the United States of America

Unhindered

Aligning the Story
of Your Heart

—

CHARITY BYERS, Ph.D.
JOHN WALKER, Ph.D.

STUDY GUIDE

AVAIL

CONTENTS

A Note to Small Group Leaders

Thank you for stepping into the role of small group leader in this journey through the *Unhindered* curriculum. Over the next 12-13 weeks, your group will delve more deeply than ever before into the beliefs, truths, and strategies that lie inside your hearts.

As you lead, keep in mind that everyone in your group is at a different place in this journey. Some participants may be extremely comfortable—even eager—to share the contents of their hearts. They may be in a place of relative health, able to share and examine their lives openly with others. On the other hand, some participants may not be as open to sharing. Many will be examining and unearthing past wounds, fears, and painful moments from the earliest days in their lives. Everyone around your circle is coming from a different context, and is at a different stage in their healing process—in their search for the unhindered life God has specifically for them. Since this study covers extremely sensitive, heart-level subjects, we encourage you to be understanding, patient, and considerate of where each group member is in their journey. The more you model vulnerability for those in your group, the more they'll be free to open up and share in the same way. Here are some brief guidelines to help you as you lead discussion and study time:

- **Make space for everyone to share.** Don't allow the few to monopolize the conversation. Sometimes, an empty silence is what a group member needs to process, prepare, and share with others.

- **Don't force anyone to share.** The biggest contribution you may give someone is the time and space to consider their own heart without saying anything. Just because someone isn't speaking doesn't mean they're not participating.

- **Make it clear that your group is a confidential space.** No group member should be speaking with those outside the group about any part of your discussion. This is standard practice in both counseling sessions and larger-scale recovery meetings, and it will elevate the authenticity of your time together. Make it clear that nothing said in the group leaves the group.

- **Start your preparation time with prayer and seeking the Lord.** What does He want to show you and your group? God knows each heart around your table, so seek Him as you prepare to lead, knowing that He already has specific purposes for your time together.

- **You're not responsible for each person's healing journey.** As much as you desire to serve and help those in your group, know that each person's journey to an unhindered life is ultimately between him- or herself and God. You can be a powerful influence in that journey for the good; but don't hold yourself accountable for the decisions, emotions, and lives of others. Focus on living YOUR unhindered life, and pour into your group out of that freedom!

Once again, thank you for serving as a group leader. We pray this study encourages, enlightens, and brings your group together in a unity you've never experienced! As we take steps toward the unhindered life God has for us, we'll become even more grateful for the community of believers around us! May this study help you take the next step in your walk with Jesus Christ, and inspire others to do the same.

Introduction

"God is willing—no, He longs—to edit your story, to replace fear with faith, doubt with confidence, and resentment with love. The astounding truth is that God will heal your deepest wounds and turn them into your greatest strengths—they become the source of your genius."

Have you ever thought of your life as a story? How do you think this perspective can reveal new insights in your journey toward an unhindered, free life?

_____

_____

_____

_____

_____

_____

_____

_____

_____

_____

_____

_____

_____

_____

_____

_____

_____

_____

_____

_____

_____

_____

_____

REFLECT ON

Read Genesis 1:26-31:

"Then God said, 'Let us make man in our image, after our like-ness. And let them have dominion over the fish of the sea and over the birds of the heavens and over the livestock and over all the earth and over every creeping thing that creeps on the earth.'

So God created man in his own image, in the image of God he created him; male and female he created them.

And God blessed them. And God said to them, 'Be fruitful and multiply and fill the earth and subdue it, and have dominion over the fish of the sea and over the birds of the heavens and over every living thing that moves on the earth.' And God said, 'Behold, I have given you every plant yielding seed that is on the face of all the earth, and every tree with seed in its fruit. You shall have them for food. And to every beast of the earth and to every bird of the heavens and to everything that creeps on the earth, everything that has the breath of life, I have given every green plant for food.' And it was so. And God saw everything that he had made, and behold, it was very good. And there was evening and there was morning, the sixth day."

Are there any areas of your life that you know need editing right now? What are they?

_____

_____

_____

_____

_____

_____

_____

_____

What's the significance of the fact that we were created in God's image? What does this reveal about the story God intends for our lives?

_____

_____

_____

_____

_____

_____

_____

_____

_____

_____

How does God's story for your life differ from the narrative that you've told yourself, or the narrative that others have spoken over you in the past?

_____

_____

_____

_____

_____

_____

_____

_____

_____

_____

"Is the shalom story of your heart still possible? You can't go back to the Garden, but you can invite God to edit your existing story so that it more closely resembles His original intentions."

What have been the biggest shapers of the story of your heart to date? Which influences have left the biggest impressions on you?

_____

_____

_____

_____

_____

_____

Why is it so essential for an author's work to be edited, proofread, and laid out before publication? What would happen if none of these preliminary steps took place?

_____

_____

_____

_____

_____

_____

Why do you think it's so easy to try to take the pen of our story into our own hands—or even to hand it to someone other than God?

_____

_____

_____

_____

_____

_____

_____

Think about the top barriers that are holding you back from your unhindered story. What are they?

_____

_____

_____

_____

_____

_____

_____

_____

_____

_____

_____

How does free will get in the way of God editing our stories? Why do you think God insisted on giving us free will anyway?

_____

_____

_____

_____

_____

_____

_____

_____

_____

_____

_____

In your own words, explain how the story of your heart determines the trajectory of your life.

_____

_____

_____

_____

_____

_____

_____

_____

_____

_____

_____

_____

Who in your life can provide a safe, supportive space while you do the work of surrendering your heart's story to God? Who will be a nonjudgmental, encouraging influence?

_____

_____

_____

_____

_____

_____

ACTION STEP: Write out a list of the areas in your life where you sense God wants to edit your story with His truth, peace, healing, and encouragement.

_____

_____

_____

_____

_____

_____

WRITING ASSIGNMENT: Write out a prayer asking for God's help as you embark on this journey to an unhindered life. Even now, ask that He would reveal to you the spaces of your heart that He wants to edit and heal. Surrender to Him, trusting that He knows best, and asking Him to take control as you begin this journey.

_____

_____

_____

_____

_____

_____

_____

_____

_____

_____

_____

_____

_____

_____

_____

_____

_____

_____

_____

_____

_____

_____

_____

_____

The Story of Your Heart

"As you've interpreted meaning through the interactions and circumstances, words were written on your heart. Before long, you began to draw conclusions and define meaning. As accumulated experiences affirmed this meaning, the words grew into themes, sentences, and chapters. The writing continued until one day a dominant story emerged, a story that carries your deepest meanings. It's the story of your heart."

Read Chapter 1 in *Unhindered*, and reflect on the questions and discuss your answers with your study group.

What influences, relationships, and experiences have helped to shape the story of your heart?

_____

_____

_____

_____

_____

_____

_____

_____

_____

_____

_____

_____

_____

_____

_____

_____

_____

_____

_____

_____

_____

_____

_____

_____

_____

_____

_____

_____

_____

REFLECT ON

Read John 10:7-16:

"So Jesus again said to them, 'Truly, truly, I say to you, I am the door of the sheep. All who came before me are thieves and robbers, but the sheep did not listen to them. I am the door. If anyone enters by me, he will be saved and will go in and out and find pasture. The thief comes only to steal and kill and destroy. I came that they may have life and have it abundantly. I am the good shepherd. The good shepherd lays down his life for the sheep. He who is a hired hand and not a shepherd, who does not own the sheep, sees the wolf coming and leaves the sheep and flees, and the wolf snatches them and scatters them. He flees because he is a hired hand and cares nothing for the sheep. I am the good shepherd. I know my own and my own know me, just as the Father knows me and I know the Father; and I lay down my life for the sheep. And I have other sheep that are not of this fold. I must bring them also, and they will listen to my voice. So there will be one flock, one shepherd. For this reason the Father loves me, because I lay down my life that I may take it up again. No one takes it from me, but I lay it down of my own accord. I have authority to lay it down, and I have authority to take it up again. This charge I have received from my Father.'"

What are some of the "words" that have been written on your heart as a result of these relationships? For example, if you had loving, supportive parents, you may have had the word "worthy" or "loved" written on your heart.

_____

_____

_____

_____

_____

_____

_____

How does Jesus' role as our Good Shepherd—our Guide—relate to uncovering the story of our heart? Why do we need His help?

_____

_____

_____

_____

_____

How does it make you feel to know that Jesus understands you better than you understand yourself?

_____

_____

_____

_____

Explain the two versions of your story that are competing for ownership of your heart.

_____

_____

_____

_____

_____

_____

_____

_____

_____

_____

_____

How, specifically, is your current story holding you back from the unhindered life God has for you?

_____

_____

_____

_____

_____

_____

_____

Do you feel that it's worthwhile to examine the story of your heart? Why or why not?

_____

_____

_____

_____

_____

_____

Why is sin only part of the reason for our flaws and dysfunctions? Does this change your perspective on the barriers in your path towards wholeness and freedom?

_____

_____

_____

_____

_____

_____

From the list on page 31, which of these hindrances do you most closely resonate with right now? Why do you think that is?

_____

_____

_____

_____

_____

_____

_____

Which of the "gaps" in this chapter do you identify with currently? Which category are most of your personal "gaps" located in (relational, spiritual, etc.)?

_____

_____

_____

_____

_____

_____

_____

In your own words, explain why being a healthy person is not a static condition, but a state of change.

_____

_____

_____

_____

_____

_____

_____

The Hindered Heart

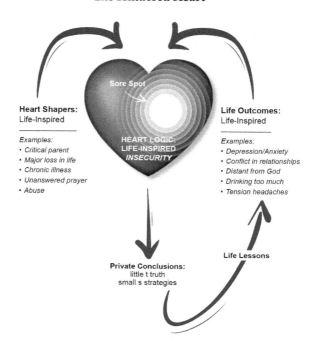

Heart Shapers:
Life-Inspired

Examples:
• Critical parent
• Major loss in life
• Chronic illness
• Unanswered prayer
• Abuse

Sore Spot

**HEART LOGIC:
LIFE-INSPIRED
INSECURITY**

Life Outcomes:
Life-Inspired

Examples:
• Depression/Anxiety
• Conflict in relationships
• Distant from God
• Drinking too much
• Tension headaches

Private Conclusions:
little t truth
small s strategies

Life Lessons

The Unhindered Heart

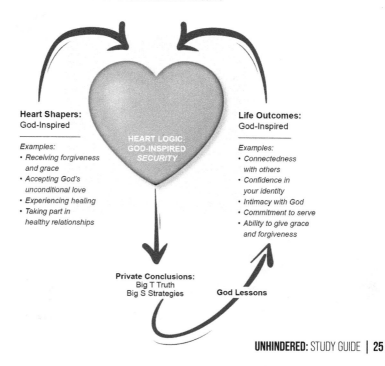

Heart Shapers:
God-Inspired

Examples:
• Receiving forgiveness
  and grace
• Accepting God's
  unconditional love
• Experiencing healing
• Taking part in
  healthy relationships

**HEART LOGIC:
GOD-INSPIRED
SECURITY**

Life Outcomes:
God-Inspired

Examples:
• Connectedness
  with others
• Confidence in
  your identity
• Intimacy with God
• Commitment to serve
• Ability to give grace
  and forgiveness

Private Conclusions:
Big T Truth
Big S Strategies

God Lessons

ACTION STEP: Take a look at the list of things that hinder us on page 31. Write down 2-3 words or ideas that resonate with where you feel held back in your life. Next, go to the Word and see what God has to say about these things. Find verses that speak to your situation and struggles; how does God's Word speak life and healing over your struggles?

_____

_____

_____

_____

_____

_____

_____

_____

_____

_____

WRITING ASSIGNMENT: Which "gaps" have made the biggest difference in your own life? Emotional gaps? Spiritual gaps? Write a few sentences about why you chose this category. What's holding you back from living an unhindered life in this area?

Heart Shapers

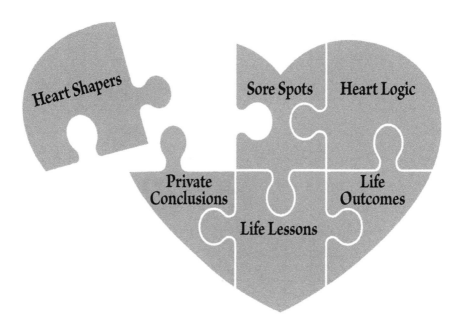

"Heart Shapers inevitably make marks on
your heart. They either write more clearly the
powerful and beautiful story God has for you, or
they distort the truth of God's love, forgiveness,
power, and joy, leaving you insecure, frantic, and
defensive. It all depends on who holds the pen."

READING TIME

Read Chapter 2 in *Unhindered,* and reflect on the questions and discuss your answers with your study group.

What influence does your heart have on the story that you tell yourself? How might this influence be downplayed (or over-played) in our world today?

_____

_____

_____

_____

_____

_____

_____

_____

_____

_____

_____

_____

_____

_____

_____

_____

_____

_____

_____

_____

_____

_____

_____

_____

_____

REFLECT ON

Read 2 Corinthians 5:14-21:

"For the love of Christ controls us, because we have concluded this: that one has died for all, therefore all have died; and he died for all, that those who live might no longer live for themselves but for him who for their sake died and was raised.

From now on, therefore, we regard no one according to the flesh. Even though we once regarded Christ according to the flesh, we regard him thus no longer. Therefore, if anyone is in Christ, he is a new creation. The old has passed away; behold, the new has come. All this is from God, who through Christ reconciled us to himself and gave us the ministry of reconciliation; that is, in Christ God was reconciling the world to himself, not counting their trespasses against them, and entrusting to us the message of reconciliation. Therefore, we are ambassadors for Christ, God making his appeal through us. We implore you on behalf of Christ, be reconciled to God. For our sake he made him to be sin who knew no sin, so that in him we might become the righteousness of God."

In this chapter, we'll take an in-depth look at the Heart Shapers that influence the story of your heart. Write a short prayer asking God to open your heart to the insights and changes He wants to make.

_____

_____

_____

_____

_____

_____

We are new creations living in a fallen world. How does this dichotomy influence how we pursue an unhindered life?

_____

_____

_____

_____

_____

_____

Why does our identity as "new creations" supersede the fallen world that we live in?

_____

_____

_____

_____

_____

_____

_____

SHARE YOUR STORY

"Those who have great faith have the courage to be ruthlessly honest—with God, with themselves, and with at least one other person—about their internal battles."

Which of the five primary Heart Shapers do you see at work in your own life? How so?

_____

_____

_____

_____

_____

_____

Which of the five secondary Heart Shapers do you see at work in your own life? How so?

_____

_____

_____

_____

_____

_____

How has experience taught your heart what to believe? What relationships, circumstances, and impressions have influenced your Heart Shapers?

_____

_____

_____

_____

_____

Explain the importance of learning to process pain in a healthy, positive way. What happens when we don't have this ability?

_____

_____

_____

_____

_____

Which of the six myths in this chapter do you find yourself believing? What do you think has contributed to this belief?

_____

_____

_____

_____

_____

Why is it difficult for you to believe God over the tangible reality of your everyday life? How does His intangibility contribute to entertaining negative Heart Shapers?

_____

_____

_____

_____

_____

_____

_____

_____

_____

_____

_____

Are there any repeated wounds you can identify in your life that have compounded over time? What about isolated, one-time wounds that have been significant?

_____

_____

_____

_____

_____

_____

_____

_____

_____

_____

_____

_____

ACTION STEP: Make a timeline of these influences, remembering that some of them may not necessarily be linked to a certain place or time. How does this timeline help you visualize and understand your Heart Shapers more fully?

_____

_____

_____

_____

_____

_____

_____

_____

_____

_____

_____

WRITING ASSIGNMENT: Write a prayer, offering the primary Heart Shaper and secondary Heart Shaper you identified in an earlier question to God. Ask Him to reveal the good, true, healthy parts of these Heart Shapers, and the elements in them that aren't in line with His will for your unhindered life!

_____

_____

_____

_____

_____

_____

_____

_____

_____

_____

_____

_____

_____

_____

_____

_____

_____

_____

_____

_____

_____

_____

_____

_____

_____

_____

Sore Spots

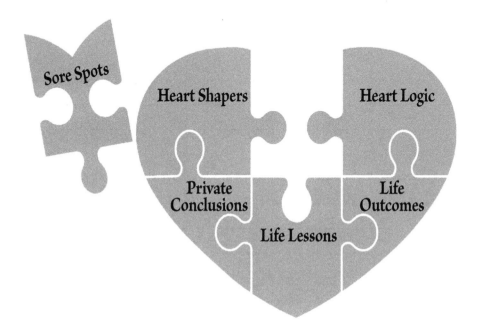

"When you experience Heart Shapers that don't reflect God's love, wisdom, and strength, they hurt, and they leave bruises on your heart we call Sore Spots. A Sore Spot is the site of your wound, the place where pain has made a home. When a Sore Spot is formed, your heart's story is altered, deviating from God's gracious intentions."

READING TIME

Read Chapter 3 in *Unhindered*, and reflect on the questions and discuss your answers with your study group.

How have the Heart Shapers we explored in the last chapter held you back from the unhindered life God has for you?

_____

_____

_____

_____

_____

_____

_____

_____

_____

_____

_____

_____

_____

_____

_____

_____

_____

_____

_____

_____

_____

_____

_____

_____

_____

REFLECT ON

Read Numbers 13:25-33:

"At the end of forty days they returned from spying out the land. And they came to Moses and Aaron and to all the congregation of the people of Israel in the wilderness of Paran, at Kadesh. They brought back word to them and to all the congregation, and showed them the fruit of the land. And they told him, 'We came to the land to which you sent us. It flows with milk and honey, and this is its fruit. However, the people who dwell in the land are strong, and the cities are fortified and very large. And besides, we saw the descendants of Anak there. The Amalekites dwell in the land of the Negeb. The Hittites, the Jebusites, and the Amorites dwell in the hill country. And the Canaanites dwell by the sea, and along the Jordan.'

But Caleb quieted the people before Moses and said, 'Let us go up at once and occupy it, for we are well able to overcome it.' Then the men who had gone up with him said, 'We are not able to go up against the people, for they are stronger than we are.' So they brought to the people of Israel a bad report of the land that they had spied out, saying, 'The land, through which we have gone to spy it out, is a land that devours its inhabitants, and all the people that we saw in it are of great height. And there we saw the Nephilim (the sons of Anak, who come from the Nephilim), and we seemed to ourselves like grasshoppers, and so we seemed to them.'"

Why do you think it's often easier to ignore those Heart Shapers instead of addressing and healing them?

_____

_____

_____

_____

_____

_____

_____

How does the ten spies' response reveal the Heart Shapers and Sore Spots inside them?

_____

_____

_____

_____

_____

_____

What about the responses of Caleb and Joshua? What does it reveal about their hearts?

_____

_____

_____

_____

_____

_____

Which of the six common Sore Spots do you resonate with the most? Why do you think this is?

_____

_____

_____

_____

_____

_____

_____

_____

_____

_____

_____

Do you tend to have an overly-emotional response to your Sore Spots, or a lack of emotion?

_____

_____

_____

_____

_____

_____

_____

_____

_____

_____

_____

_____

How do Sore Spots inevitably affect our entire lives, even if they only exist within a portion of our hearts?

_____

_____

_____

_____

_____

_____

_____

_____

How do your Sore Spots influence your interpretation of who you are, and the life that you live?

_____

_____

_____

_____

_____

_____

_____

_____

_____

_____

_____

_____

_____

_____

_____

_____

_____

_____

_____

_____

_____

_____

_____

_____

_____

_____

_____

_____

_____

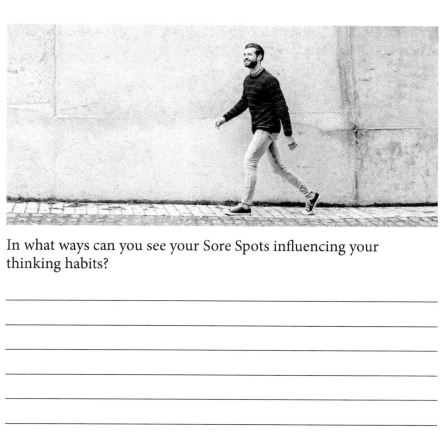

In what ways can you see your Sore Spots influencing your thinking habits?

_____

_____

_____

_____

_____

_____

_____

_____

How about your emotions? What difference do your Sore Spots make in your feelings and the way you experience them?

_____

_____

_____

_____

_____

_____

_____

_____

ACTION STEP: Draw your own Sore Spot diagram, using the one on page 92-93 as an example.

Do your Sore Spots take up a majority of the space in your heart? Or are they relatively small, impacting you only marginally on a daily basis?

_____

_____

_____

_____

_____

_____

_____

_____

_____

_____

_____

WRITING ASSIGNMENT: How have you seen the influence of your Sore Spots manifest in your life? Choose one or two to focus on and reflect on how they've impacted your life and kept you from living in the unhindered way that God has for you. Spend some time in prayer asking God to help you understand these Sore Spots more fully, without feelings of condemnation, shame, or guilt.

_____

_____

_____

_____

_____

_____

_____

_____

_____

_____

_____

_____

Sore Spots as the Source of Genius

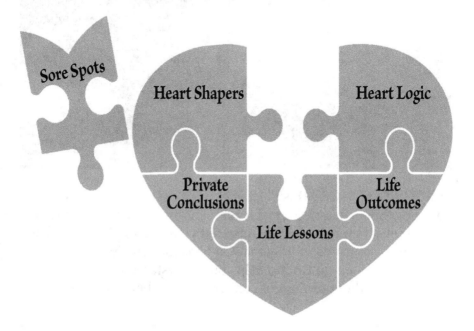

"The site of your wound can become the source of your genius—the very best of you."

Read Chapter 4 in *Unhindered*, and reflect on the questions and discuss your answers with your study group.

How have you already seen God use your flaws, weaknesses, and shortcomings for His glory and your good?

_____

_____

_____

_____

_____

_____

_____

_____

_____

_____

_____

_____

_____

_____

_____

_____

_____

_____

_____

_____

_____

_____

_____

_____

_____

_____

REFLECT ON

Read John 21:15-19:

"When they had finished breakfast, Jesus said to Simon Peter, 'Simon, son of John, do you love me more than these?' He said to him, 'Yes, Lord; you know that I love you.' He said to him, 'Feed my lambs.' He said to him a second time, 'Simon, son of John, do you love me?' He said to him, 'Yes, Lord; you know that I love you.' He said to him, 'Tend my sheep.' He said to him the third time, 'Simon, son of John, do you love me?' Peter was grieved because he said to him the third time, 'Do you love me?' and he said to him, 'Lord, you know everything; you know that I love you.' Jesus said to him, 'Feed my sheep. Truly, truly, I say to you, when you were young, you used to dress yourself and walk wherever you wanted, but when you are old, you will stretch out your hands, and another will dress you and carry you where you do not want to go.' (This he said to show by what kind of death he was to glorify God.) And after saying this he said to him, 'Follow me.'"

How do we see God using His people's Sore Spots to further His
plans throughout Scripture? Can you think of a few examples?

_____

_____

_____

_____

_____

_____

How did Peter's denial of Christ, and his restoration, serve to
enhance his ministry in the New Testament?

_____

_____

_____

_____

_____

_____

How did Jesus' approach in this passage help to heal Peter and
restore his heart?

_____

_____

_____

_____

_____

_____

*"Becoming
aware of
Sore Spots
isn't about
becoming
hyper-
focused on
the pain.
It's just the
opposite.
Acknowl-
edging Sore
Spots is a
means of
healing
them so you
can take
the focus off
them! It's
the path to
freedom."*

Why is it essential to honestly evaluate our Sore Spots if we're going to live the unhindered life that God has for us?

_____

_____

_____

_____

_____

_____

_____

Which of the "Source of Genius" stories in this chapter resonates with you the most, and why?

_____

_____

_____

_____

_____

_____

_____

Why is pain a good indicator of where the Sore Spots in our hearts are located?

_____

_____

_____

_____

_____

_____

_____

The Sore Spot Has Taken Over

Lots of Room Left for God's Beautifully Edited Story

Why do you think we often assume that supernatural healing will be instantaneous? What are the benefits of God leading us through a healing process, rather than condensing that process into a single moment?

_____

How would your life look different today if there were no Sore Spots in your heart? What understanding, maturity, or other insights wouldn't you have if this were the case?

_____

_____

_____

_____

_____

_____

_____

_____

_____

_____

_____

What's the hardest part for you about identifying and acknowledging your Sore Spots?

_____

_____

_____

_____

_____

_____

_____

_____

_____

_____

_____

ACTION STEP: What strength does God want to use to replace your Sore Spot? Find one or two Bible verses to underscore His truth in this area. Put these verses up somewhere you will see them every day, so that they can encourage you and remind you of His truth!

_____

_____

_____

_____

_____

_____

_____

_____

_____

_____

_____

_____

WRITING ASSIGNMENT: After reading this chapter, identify some of the alternative desires God has for your heart, as opposed to the negative Heart Shapers and Sore Spots that have influenced you. Take time to invite God into those painful places in your heart so that He would begin to show you His perspective. Take time to sit in silence and allow His perfect will for you to become clearer and more real!

Heart Logic: Unpacking the Four Questions

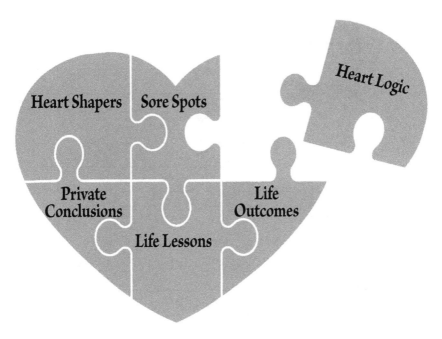

"*Heart Logic is established very early in life. It can be revised, but your initial conclusions are often written deep in your heart, making them hard to rewrite.*"

Read Chapter 5 in *Unhindered*, and reflect on the questions and discuss your answers with your study group.

How would you answer these four questions? Remember, be authentic and honest with yourself—write the first answer that comes to mind.

1. God: Is God good? Is He really good all the time?

_____

_____

_____

_____

_____

_____

_____

_____

_____

_____

_____

_____

_____

_____

_____

_____

_____

_____

_____

_____

_____

_____

_____

REFLECT ON

Read Romans 5:1-11:

"Therefore, since we have been justified by faith, we have peace with God through our Lord Jesus Christ. Through him we have also obtained access by faith into this grace in which we stand, and we rejoice in hope of the glory of God. Not only that, but we rejoice in our sufferings, knowing that suffering produces endurance, and endurance produces character, and character produces hope, and hope does not put us to shame, because God's love has been poured into our hearts through the Holy Spirit who has been given to us.

For while we were still weak, at the right time Christ died for the ungodly. For one will scarcely die for a righteous person— though perhaps for a good person one would dare even to die— but God shows his love for us in that while we were still sinners, Christ died for us. Since, therefore, we have now been justified by his blood, much more shall we be saved by him from the wrath of God. For if while we were enemies we were reconciled to God by the death of his Son, much more, now that we are reconciled, shall we be saved by his life. More than that, we also rejoice in God through our Lord Jesus Christ, through whom we have now received reconciliation."

2. Yourself: Am I good even though I'm flawed? Am I truly valued and worthy of love?

_____

_____

_____

_____

_____

_____

_____

_____

3. Other people: Are other people good? Is there goodness among the brokenness in humanity?

_____

_____

_____

_____

_____

_____

_____

_____

4. The world: Is life good? Is life good even in the most difficult times?

_____

_____

_____

_____

_____

_____

Looking back at your answers, how do you think the Heart Shapers and Sore Spots we've explored in previous chapters have influenced your beliefs?

_____

_____

_____

_____

_____

_____

_____

What role does suffering play in the Christian life, according to this passage?

_____

_____

_____

_____

_____

_____

_____

_____

_____

_____

_____

How does this perspective go against some of the messages that today's Christian culture would have us believe? How does God work differently in us than we sometimes think He does?

_____

_____

_____

_____

_____

_____

_____

_____

_____

_____

_____

In your own words, explain what Heart Logic is and what effect it has on you.

_____

_____

_____

_____

_____

_____

_____

_____

_____

_____

_____

Why do you think our Heart Logic often exists undetected, beneath our radar?

_____

_____

_____

_____

_____

_____

_____

_____

_____

_____

_____

_____

Which of the four questions in this chapter caught your attention? Did any of your answers surprise you? How so?

_____

_____

_____

_____

_____

What purpose has God provided in the midst of your pain? What opportunities has He brought to your attention?

_____

_____

_____

_____

_____

How does a realization of our flaws change our perspective on God and His grace?

_____

_____

_____

_____

_____

How do you think answering the four Heart Logic questions connects to our capacity to hope and trust (both God and other people)?

_____

_____

_____

_____

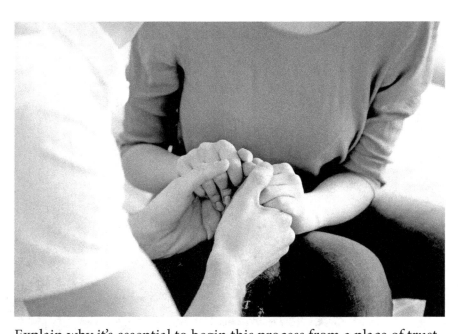

Explain why it's essential to begin this process from a place of trust. Why can't we have an unhindered life without trust?

_____

_____

_____

_____

How does saying "Yes" to the Heart Logic Questions renew our hope?

_____

_____

_____

_____

ACTION STEP: Who do you know that is able to say "yes" to any of the four Heart Logic questions you aren't currently able to answer "yes" to? If at all possible, spend some time with this person—over the phone, in person, or on video chat—and ask the Holy Spirit to help this time influence your heart and move you towards being able to say "yes" to that question.

WRITING ASSIGNMENT: Write a prayer, asking God to help you as you journey towards being able to say "yes" authentically to all four Heart Logic questions. Be honest with Him about areas you aren't currently able to say "yes" in, asking for His continued revelation as to what's holding you back!

_____

_____

_____

_____

_____

_____

_____

_____

_____

_____

_____

_____

_____

_____

_____

_____

_____

_____

_____

_____

_____

_____

_____

_____

_____

Heart Logic: Correcting Flawed Assumptions

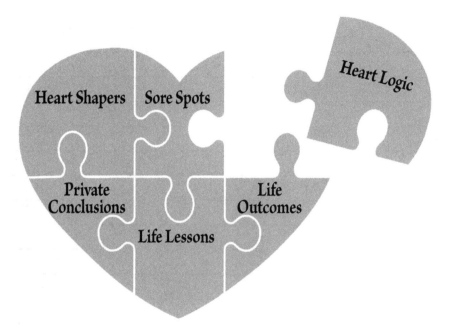

"The "yeses" we give to the Heart Logic questions can't be superficial or rote; they must be genuine. Fear keeps us from honesty, but we have a God who knows the worst about us and loves us still. We can trust Him."

READING TIME

Read Chapter 6 in *Unhindered*, and reflect on the questions and discuss your answers with your study group.

How does Christian culture today try to give quick, easy answers to the Heart Logic questions without truly delving beneath the surface?

_____

_____

_____

_____

_____

_____

_____

_____

_____

_____

What about you personally? Have you been tempted to simply answer "yes" to the questions without truly meaning it? Why or why not?

_____

_____

_____

_____

_____

_____

_____

_____

REFLECT ON

Read Psalm 139:

"O LORD, you have searched me and known me!
You know when I sit down and when I rise up;
  you discern my thoughts from afar.
You search out my path and my lying down
  and are acquainted with all my ways.
Even before a word is on my tongue,
  behold, O LORD, you know it altogether.
You hem me in, behind and before,
  and lay your hand upon me.
Such knowledge is too wonderful for me;
  it is high; I cannot attain it.
Where shall I go from your Spirit?
  Or where shall I flee from your presence?
If I ascend to heaven, you are there!
  If I make my bed in Sheol, you are there!
If I take the wings of the morning
  and dwell in the uttermost parts of the sea,
even there your hand shall lead me,
  and your right hand shall hold me.
If I say, "Surely the darkness shall cover me,
  and the light about me be night,"
even the darkness is not dark to you;
  the night is bright as the day,
  for darkness is as light with you.
For you formed my inward parts;
  you knitted me together in my mother's womb.
I praise you, for I am fearfully and wonderfully made.
Wonderful are your works;
  my soul knows it very well.
My frame was not hidden from you,
when I was being made in secret,
  intricately woven in the depths of the earth.
Your eyes saw my unformed substance;
in your book were written, every one of them,
  the days that were formed for me,

when as yet there was none of them.
How precious to me are your thoughts, O God!
  How vast is the sum of them!
If I would count them, they are more than the sand.
  I awake, and I am still with you.
Oh that you would slay the wicked, O God!
  O men of blood, depart from me!
They speak against you with malicious intent;
  your enemies take your name in vain.
Do I not hate those who hate you, O LORD?
  And do I not loathe those who rise up against you?
I hate them with complete hatred;
  I count them my enemies.
Search me, O God, and know my heart!
  Try me and know my thoughts!
And see if there be any grievous way in me,
  and lead me in the way everlasting!"

What revelations of God's character and love for you do you find in this passage?

_____

_____

_____

_____

_____

_____

_____

_____

_____

_____

_____

_____

_____

_____

SHARE YOUR STORY

"You can't cross your gap if the funda-mental conclusions you've drawn— about who you are, who God is, who people are, and what this world is— don't align with God's promises."

Why is it important to the process of becoming unhindered that God knows us better than we know ourselves?

_____

_____

_____

_____

_____

_____

_____

_____

_____

_____

_____

Do you find it hard to trust in God's good-ness in the midst of difficult situations? Explain your answer.

_____

_____

_____

_____

_____

_____

_____

_____

_____

_____

_____

_____

Where do we end up going for security, worth, and identity when we don't believe in God's goodness? Where do you personally end up going for these things?

_____

_____

_____

_____

_____

_____

_____

_____

_____

_____

_____

_____

_____

_____

_____

Why do you think God often chooses to walk with us through our pain rather than delivering us from it immediately?

_____

_____

_____

_____

_____

_____

Which of the three phases of Heart Logic do you think has had the biggest impact on the story of your heart? Why?

_____

_____

_____

_____

_____

_____

_____

_____

_____

_____

_____

_____

What corrective experiences have you had since accepting Christ as your Lord and Savior? How have these experiences deepened your understanding of who God is, who you are, what humanity is, and what life is all about?

_____

_____

_____

_____

_____

_____

_____

_____

_____

_____

_____

What do you find most difficult about acknowledging your faulty Heart Logic at this point in the study (keeping in mind that correcting it may require you to face the healing process as a result of perceived injustices, an incredible loss, an unanswered prayer, and other painful experiences)?

_____

_____

_____

_____

_____

_____

_____

_____

_____

_____

_____

ACTION STEP: How are you going to choose to edit your faulty Heart Logic, after reaching this point in the study? What areas in particular need to be addressed? How will you practically go about partnering with the Holy Spirit to address these areas?

_____

_____

_____

_____

_____

_____

_____

_____

_____

_____

_____

_____

_____

_____

_____

_____

_____

_____

_____

_____

_____

_____

_____

_____

_____

_____

_____

_____

_____

WRITING ASSIGNMENT: Write a short prayer asking God for forgiveness for the times you've chosen other sources to define your fundamental views. Ask Him for His help in trusting that He is good, and coming to Him first, no matter what.

chapter 7

Private Conclusions and Life Lessons

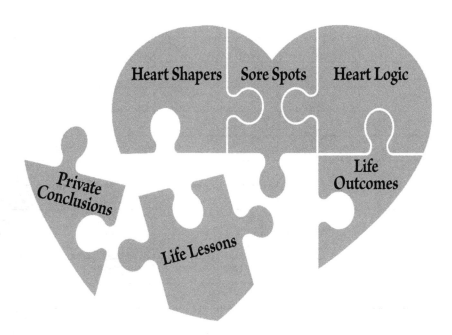

"The longer you live with your existing Private Conclusions, the more you settle into self-defeating ways of thinking and being."

READING TIME

Read Chapter 7 in *Unhindered,* and reflect on the questions and discuss your answers with your study group.

Consider your answers from the previous chapters about Heart Shapers, Sore Spots, and Heart Logic that have led you to where you are today. What connections do you see? (You can also refer to the Appendix to help you reflect on what you've learned so far.)

_____

_____

_____

_____

_____

_____

_____

_____

_____

_____

_____

_____

_____

_____

_____

_____

_____

_____

_____

_____

_____

_____

REFLECT ON

Read Isaiah 58:6-12:

"Is not this the fast that I choose:
to loose the bonds of wickedness,
to undo the straps of the yoke,
to let the oppressed go free,
and to break every yoke?
Is it not to share your bread with the hungry
and bring the homeless poor into your house;
when you see the naked, to cover him,
and not to hide yourself from your own flesh?
Then shall your light break forth like the dawn,
and your healing shall spring up speedily;
your righteousness shall go before you;
the glory of the LORD shall be your rear guard.
Then you shall call, and the LORD will answer;
you shall cry, and he will say, 'Here I am.'
If you take away the yoke from your midst,
the pointing of the finger, and speaking wickedness,
if you pour yourself out for the hungry
and satisfy the desire of the afflicted,
then shall your light rise in the darkness
and your gloom be as the noonday.
And the LORD will guide you continually
and satisfy your desire in scorched places
and make your bones strong;
and you shall be like a watered garden,
like a spring of water,
whose waters do not fail.
And your ancient ruins shall be rebuilt;
you shall raise up the foundations of many generations;
you shall be called the repairer of the breach,
the restorer of streets to dwell in."

What conclusions have these things led you to believe personally, either about yourself, God, or the world?

_____

_____

_____

_____

_____

_____

In this passage, God calls His people to a higher form of living than simply fasting and sacrificing for the sake of doing so. He wants their hearts to become more like His! What stands out to you about the life God wants for His people in this passage?

_____

_____

_____

_____

_____

_____

How did the Israelites' faulty Private Conclusions probably contribute to their deviance from God's will in this passage? What beliefs were holding them back from the unhindered life God had for them?

_____

_____

_____

_____

_____

_____

*"The rules
you adopt
as your
guidebook
are an accu-
mulation of
the Private
Conclusions
swirling
around
inside of
you."*

In your own words, define little t truths. How do they influence your worldview and self-perception?

_____

_____

_____

_____

_____

_____

_____

_____

What little t truths are you currently holding in your heart? Were you conscious of them before reading this chapter?

_____

_____

_____

_____

_____

_____

_____

_____

_____

_____

_____

_____

_____

_____

_____

What part of God's Word have you "made yourself an exception to" (look at The Two Gospels Syndrome portion of the chapter)? Why do you think you've done this?

_____

_____

_____

_____

_____

_____

_____

_____

_____

_____

_____

What are small s strategies, and how do they reveal our Sore Spots and faulty Heart Logic?

_____

_____

_____

_____

_____

_____

_____

_____

_____

_____

_____

Which small s strategies have you adopted, either consciously or subconsciously? How do you think these strategies helped you to survive in a set of past circumstances, and how do they not work so well for you now that your circumstances have changed?

_____

_____

_____

_____

_____

_____

_____

_____

_____

_____

_____

Have you adopted any little t truths or small s strategies that line up with God's truth? What are they?

_____

_____

_____

_____

_____

_____

_____

_____

_____

_____

_____

_____

Explain why a strategy can be a "good thing gone wrong." Have you experienced this in your own walk with the Lord? How so?

_____

_____

_____

_____

_____

_____

_____

_____

_____

_____

_____

_____

ACTION STEP: Make a list of all the little t truths and small s strategies in your heart currently that align with God's Word. Then, make a list of the truths and strategies that don't align with His Word. Find Scripture verses for each set of truths and strategies that reinforce what God says, and add them to this list.

_____

_____

_____

_____

_____

_____

_____

_____

_____

_____

_____

_____

_____

_____

WRITING ASSIGNMENT: Write a prayer thanking God for the clarity He's already brought to your journey. Ask Him to help you understand your heart and everything that has influenced it—all the answers you've written so far—in a way that reflects His own love for and unconditional acceptance of you. Ask for His perspective on the discoveries you're making!

_____

_____

_____

_____

_____

_____

_____

_____

_____

_____

_____

_____

_____

_____

_____

_____

_____

_____

_____

_____

_____

_____

_____

_____

_____

The Truth Will Set You Free

"God offers a new path with Big T Truth, Big S Strategies, and God Lessons that lead you across your gap into a more abundant life."

READING TIME

Read Chapter 8 in *Unhindered*, and reflect on the ques- tions and discuss your answers with your study group.

Look at the little t truths you wrote down in the last chapter. Can you find Scriptures that replace these truths with God's Big T Truth? Take a few minutes in silence to listen for God's voice and promptings—what does He want you to understand that's different from what you've always understood?

_____

_____

_____

_____

_____

_____

_____

_____

_____

_____

_____

_____

_____

_____

_____

_____

_____

_____

_____

_____

_____

REFLECT ON

Read James 1:2-18:

"Count it all joy, my brothers, when you meet trials of various kinds, for you know that the testing of your faith produces steadfastness. And let steadfastness have its full effect, that you may be perfect and complete, lacking in nothing.

If any of you lacks wisdom, let him ask God, who gives generously to all without reproach, and it will be given him. But let him ask in faith, with no doubting, for the one who doubts is like a wave of the sea that is driven and tossed by the wind. For that person must not suppose that he will receive anything from the Lord; he is a double-minded man, unstable in all his ways.

Let the lowly brother boast in his exaltation, and the rich in his humiliation, because like a flower of the grass he will pass away. For the sun rises with its scorching heat and withers the grass; its flower falls, and its beauty perishes. So also will the rich man fade away in the midst of his pursuits.

Blessed is the man who remains steadfast under trial, for when he has stood the test he will receive the crown of life, which God has promised to those who love him. Let no one say when he is tempted, 'I am being tempted by God,' for God cannot be tempted with evil, and he himself tempts no one. But each person is tempted when he is lured and enticed by his own desire. Then desire when it has conceived gives birth to sin, and sin when it is fully grown brings forth death.

Do not be deceived, my beloved brothers. Every good gift and every perfect gift is from above, coming down from the Father of lights, with whom there is no variation or shadow due to change. Of his own will he brought us forth by the word of truth, that we should be a kind of firstfruits of his creatures."

What about the small s strategies you identified in Chapter 7—what Bible verses can you find that encourage God's Big S Strategies instead? Take a few minutes in silence to listen for God's voice and promptings—what does He want you to do that's different from what you've always done to try to be okay?

_____

_____

_____

_____

_____

_____

Do you find it easy to ask God for wisdom, and to believe that He wants to give you good and perfect gifts? Why or why not?

_____

_____

_____

_____

_____

_____

Based on this passage, what is God's heart and desire for you in light of the Sore Spots and the Heart Logic you've adopted up to this point?

_____

_____

_____

_____

_____

_____

_____

"God doesn't want to fit into your worldview; He wants to recreate your world-view."

Which of the healed Sore Spots and Big T Truth pairings in this chapter resonate most powerfully with you?

_____

_____

_____

_____

_____

_____

_____

_____

_____

_____

_____

_____

_____

_____

_____

_____

_____

_____

_____

_____

_____

_____

_____

_____

_____

_____

Explain the Nevertheless Principle, and how it's foundational to living the unhindered life God has for you.

_____

_____

_____

_____

_____

_____

_____

_____

_____

_____

Which premise for the Nevertheless Principle stands out most to you? Why do you think this is? Write out a few Nevertheless statements that apply to your life right now. What stands out to you about what you wrote down?

_____

_____

_____

_____

_____

_____

_____

_____

_____

_____

_____

_____

_____

Explain why changing your small s strategies to Big S Strategies may not change that much on the outside, or in certain outcomes. Why is it still significant that we make this exchange?

_____

_____

_____

_____

_____

_____

Which one of the Big S Strategies in this chapter stands out to you most, and why? How can you begin to practically implement this strategy, with God's help?

_____

_____

_____

_____

_____

_____

In your own words, explain the difference between enduring pain and being harmed. How do you think pain is sometimes more helpful than comfort?

_____

_____

_____

_____

_____

_____

_____

_____

_____

_____

_____

_____

_____

_____

_____

_____

_____

_____

_____

_____

_____

_____

_____

_____

What God Lessons have you gleaned from this study so far?

_____

_____

_____

_____

_____

_____

_____

_____

_____

_____

_____

_____

_____

_____

_____

_____

_____

_____

_____

_____

_____

_____

ACTION STEP: Find a Scripture verse that speaks to the most important Big T Truth in your life right now, and another for the most important Big S Strategy in your life right now. Spend some time reflecting on these verses—maybe even get a study Bible or a commentary to help you delve more deeply into their meanings!

WRITING ASSIGNMENT: Write out your Personalized Message, using the Big T Truths, Big S Strategies, and God Lessons you've uncovered up to this point. Read this message out loud, and truly open your heart to receiving the message as truth, steeped in spiritual authority, and backed by the work of Christ!

_____

_____

_____

_____

_____

_____

_____

_____

_____

_____

_____

_____

_____

_____

_____

_____

_____

_____

_____

_____

_____

_____

_____

_____

Life Outcomes: Your Story from the Outside In

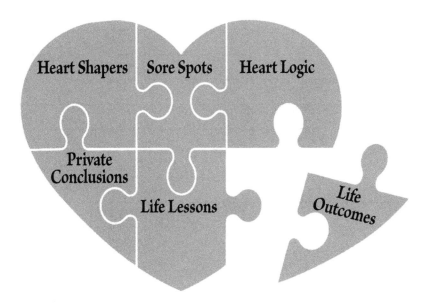

"Breaking the cycle begins in the deepest parts of our hearts. We start with the roots, going down into the depths of the heart to rewrite the story. That's the only way to get out of the rut and put yourself on an upward trajectory!"

Read Chapter 9 in *Unhindered,* and reflect on the questions and discuss your answers with your study group.

Why do you think it's so important to change the story of our heart before we try to modify our behavior? In other words, why do you think our stories are written from the inside out?

_____

_____

_____

_____

_____

_____

_____

_____

_____

_____

_____

_____

_____

_____

_____

_____

_____

_____

_____

_____

_____

_____

_____

_____

REFLECT ON

Read Isaiah 55:6-13:

"Seek the LORD while he may be found;
call upon him while he is near;
let the wicked forsake his way,
and the unrighteous man his thoughts;
let him return to the LORD, that he may
have compassion on him,
and to our God, for he will abundantly pardon.
For my thoughts are not your thoughts,
neither are your ways my ways, declares the LORD.
For as the heavens are higher than the earth,
so are my ways higher than your ways
and my thoughts than your thoughts.
For as the rain and the snow come down from heaven
and do not return there but water the earth,
making it bring forth and sprout,
giving seed to the sower and bread to the eater,
so shall my word be that goes out from my mouth;
it shall not return to me empty,
but it shall accomplish that which I purpose,
and shall succeed in the thing for which I sent it.
For you shall go out in joy
and be led forth in peace;
the mountains and the hills before you
shall break forth into singing,
and all the trees of the field shall clap their hands.
Instead of the thorn shall come up the cypress;
instead of the brier shall come up the myrtle;
and it shall make a name for the LORD,
an everlasting sign that shall not be cut off."

How have you seen the story of your heart manifest outwardly—
not just through your strategies, but in the way you live your life?

_____

_____

_____

_____

_____

What encouragement or comfort do you glean from this passage?

_____

_____

_____

_____

_____

How does this passage challenge you to see yourself, and God, in a
new light?

_____

_____

_____

_____

_____

Who are the top five people in your life you can depend on as you
go about the journey of re-writing your heart's story? List them
below.

_____

_____

_____

_____

_____

"Until you rewrite the story of your heart, you'll be stuck in a rut, too. That's because our choices are a self-perpetuating cycle, and until something breaks it, it plays on repeat."

Have you tried to change your heart's story through outward means, such as fresh schedules, additional tasks, or different habits? What did you learn from these experiments?

_____

_____

_____

_____

_____

_____

_____

_____

_____

_____

_____

_____

_____

_____

_____

_____

_____

_____

_____

_____

_____

_____

_____

_____

What outcomes have been compromised in your life in the following areas?

Emotional:

_____

_____

_____

_____

_____

_____

_____

_____

_____

_____

Relational:

_____

_____

_____

_____

_____

_____

_____

_____

_____

_____

_____

Spiritual:

_____

_____

_____

_____

_____

_____

_____

_____

_____

_____

_____

_____

Behavioral:

_____

_____

_____

_____

_____

_____

_____

_____

_____

_____

_____

_____

Physical:

_____

_____

_____

_____

_____

_____

_____

_____

_____

_____

_____

_____

_____

Character:

_____

_____

_____

_____

_____

_____

_____

_____

_____

_____

_____

_____

_____

In your own words, explain how everything we have studied so far—Heart Shapers, Sore Spots, Heart Logic, Private Conclusions, and Life Lessons—fits together in writing our heart's stories.

_____

_____

_____

_____

_____

_____

_____

_____

_____

_____

_____

_____

_____

_____

_____

_____

_____

_____

_____

_____

_____

_____

_____

_____

_____

_____

_____

_____

_____

_____

_____

_____

In this chapter, find the Sore Spot chart that most closely corresponds to your current struggle. Which words in the corresponding "Heart Shapers," "Heart Logic," "little t truths," "small s strategies," and "Life Outcomes" boxes stand out to you?

_____

_____

_____

_____

_____

_____

_____

What is God showing you about what's waiting for you on the other side of unhindering your heart in the following areas?

Emotional:

_____

_____

_____

_____

Relational:

_____

_____

_____

_____

_____

_____

_____

Spiritual:

_____

_____

_____

_____

_____

_____

_____

Behavioral:

_____

_____

_____

_____

_____

_____

_____

Physical:

_____

_____

_____

_____

_____

_____

_____

Character:

_____

_____

_____

_____

_____

_____

_____

What's your role in this journey, and what can only God do as you journey towards your unhindered life?

_____

_____

_____

_____

_____

_____

_____

_____

_____

_____

ACTION STEP: What's one Life Outcome you want to see as a result of this journey to an unhindered life? What are some of the practical steps—both internal and external—you need to take to partner with God in realizing that outcome? Make a list of these steps and make a plan to begin walking them out, day by day.

_____

_____

_____

_____

_____

_____

_____

_____

_____

_____

WRITING ASSIGNMENT: Reflect and write about the Life Outcomes you've seen so far in your journey. Which outcomes have been a result of the Sore Spots you've suffered? What about redeemed outcomes—how has God brought about beauty and restoration from your obedience and godly decisions?

_____

_____

_____

_____

_____

_____

_____

_____

_____

_____

_____

_____

_____

_____

Long Obedience in a New Direction

"You have to lean into God's edits every day. It will be long and sometimes difficult, but you'll get there if you decide to stay the course."

READING TIME

Read Chapter 10 in *Unhindered,* and reflect on the ques-tions and discuss your answers with your study group.

What is going to be difficult about your daily journey towards an unhindered life? Where will you need to exercise obedience, even when it's unpleasant?

_____

_____

_____

_____

_____

_____

_____

_____

_____

_____

_____

_____

_____

_____

_____

_____

_____

_____

_____

_____

_____

_____

_____

Read Hebrews 12:7-14:

"It is for discipline that you have to endure. God is treating you as sons. For what son is there whom his father does not discipline? If you are left without discipline, in which all have participated, then you are illegitimate children and not sons. Besides this, we have had earthly fathers who disciplined us and we respected them. Shall we not much more be subject to the Father of spirits and live? For they disciplined us for a short time as it seemed best to them, but he disciplines us for our good, that we may share his holiness. For the moment all discipline seems painful rather than pleasant, but later it yields the peaceful fruit of righteousness to those who have been trained by it.

Therefore lift your drooping hands and strengthen your weak knees, and make straight paths for your feet, so that what is lame may not be put out of joint but rather be healed. Strive for peace with everyone, and for the holiness without which no one will see the Lord."

Can you think of some of the temptations that will arise as you fight toward a new life? How will your mind and heart tend to go backwards toward your old ways of living?

Explain the difference between discipline and punishment. Why is discipline essential to the Christian walk?

_____

_____

_____

_____

_____

_____

_____

_____

_____

_____

_____

Does this chapter change your perspective on what an unhindered life will look like? How so?

_____

_____

_____

_____

_____

_____

_____

_____

_____

_____

_____

_____

_____

What power does the past hold over us? How does it influence us, even as we recognize and move toward a better way of living?

_____

_____

_____

_____

_____

_____

In your own words, explain the difference between your natural self and your spiritual self. How are they distinct?

_____

_____

_____

_____

_____

Who can you depend on who has walked down this road before? What wisdom and insight does this person have to share with you from their own experiences?

_____

_____

_____

_____

_____

_____

Why doesn't transformation end when a heart is changed? How is it an ongoing process, like recovery from surgery? And what is God's purpose in doing it this way?

_____

_____

_____

_____

_____

_____

_____

_____

_____

How is the long obedience of an unhindered life different from the long obedience that we've attempted to adopt before?

_____

_____

_____

_____

_____

_____

_____

_____

_____

_____

_____

What are the two steps to being convinced of the value of your new story? What will these steps look like specifically in your own life?

_____

_____

_____

_____

_____

_____

_____

_____

_____

_____

_____

_____

_____

_____

_____

_____

_____

_____

_____

ACTION STEP: Reach out to a friend, family member, or loved one who can keep you accountable as you walk in obedience. Share one or two steps with them that God is leading you to take, and ask your loved one to keep you accountable as you walk in obedience to His voice.

WRITING ASSIGNMENT: How has God already enabled you to take concrete steps toward your unhindered story? What steps have you taken, and what were the results? What steps do you still need to take?

_____

_____

_____

_____

_____

_____

_____

_____

_____

_____

_____

_____

_____

_____

_____

_____

_____

_____

_____

_____

_____

_____

_____

Fighting the Battle

*"You're in a battle between the two stories: the
one your experiences have written and the one
God is rewriting. It's the battle to trust the right
author—your imperfect life or your perfect God."*

READING TIME

Read Chapter 11 in *Unhindered,* and reflect on the questions and discuss your answers with your study group.

What makes the journey towards an unhindered life a battle?

_____

_____

_____

_____

_____

_____

_____

_____

_____

_____

_____

_____

_____

_____

_____

_____

_____

_____

_____

_____

_____

_____

_____

_____

_____

_____

REFLECT ON

Read Ephesians 6:10-20:

"Finally, be strong in the Lord and in the strength of his might. Put on the whole armor of God, that you may be able to stand against the schemes of the devil. For we do not wrestle against flesh and blood, but against the rulers, against the authorities, against the cosmic powers over this present darkness, against the spiritual forces of evil in the heavenly places. Therefore take up the whole armor of God, that you may be able to withstand in the evil day, and having done all, to stand firm. Stand therefore, having fastened on the belt of truth, and having put on the breastplate of righteousness, and, as shoes for your feet, having put on the readiness given by the gospel of peace. In all circumstances take up the shield of faith, with which you can extinguish all the flaming darts of the evil one; and take the helmet of salvation, and the sword of the Spirit, which is the word of God, praying at all times in the Spirit, with all prayer and supplication. To that end, keep alert with all perseverance, making supplication for all the saints, and also for me, that words may be given to me in opening my mouth boldly to proclaim the mystery of the gospel, for which I am an ambassador in chains, that I may declare it boldly, as I ought to speak."

How has this battle looked in your own life already, as you've fought to move towards the better way of living God has for you?

_____

_____

_____

_____

_____

_____

_____

_____

Which piece of armor do you need most at this moment? Can you find Scriptures that remind and encourage you to put on this piece of armor?

_____

_____

_____

_____

_____

_____

_____

_____

_____

_____

_____

What piece of armor has God been cultivating and reminding you to put on? Which piece do you feel familiar with already?

_____

_____

_____

_____

_____

_____

_____

_____

_____

_____

_____

Explain the two battles taking place, and how they are unique from one another.

_____

_____

_____

_____

_____

_____

_____

What is a collision? How can it remind you of the direction you're moving in, towards an unhindered life?

_____

_____

_____

_____

_____

_____

Do you tend to have more unrecognized collisions or recognized collisions? Explain your answer.

_____

_____

_____

_____

_____

_____

How can we learn to actually embrace collisions? What are some practical steps you can take during a collision to make sure you appreciate and make the most of it?

Knowing what to look for will help us identify collisions more quickly. What are some phrases or words that represent your little t truths and small s strategies? What do they sound like?

_____

_____

_____

_____

_____

_____

_____

_____

_____

_____

_____

_____

_____

_____

_____

_____

_____

_____

ACTION STEP: What thoughts, feelings, and actions accompany a swerve back to your old way of living? Stop, think, and pray, surrendering these tendencies to God and asking for His supernatural help in overcoming them!

Thoughts:

_____

_____

_____

_____

_____

_____

_____

Feelings:

_____

_____

_____

_____

_____

_____

Actions:

_____

_____

_____

_____

_____

_____

WRITING ASSIGNMENT: In the Appendix, take some time to write out your prayer or personalized message. Feel free to use the "Aftercare Plan" in the chapter to write out your next steps. Take your time on this!

_____

_____

_____

_____

_____

_____

_____

_____

_____

_____

_____

_____

_____

_____

Living in Your New Story

"We believe God's definition of genius is living to the full capacity of your spiritual DNA. It is revealed when God's original story is returned to your heart and you cross your gap into your unhindered life."

READING TIME

Read Chapter 12 in *Unhindered*, and reflect on the questions and discuss your answers with your study group.

What are your top three takeaways from this study so far?

_____

_____

_____

_____

_____

_____

_____

_____

_____

_____

_____

_____

_____

_____

_____

_____

_____

_____

_____

_____

_____

_____

_____

_____

_____

_____

_____

_____

REFLECT ON

Read Matthew 11:25-30.

"At that time Jesus declared, 'I thank you, Father, Lord of heaven and earth, that you have hidden these things from the wise and understanding and revealed them to little children; yes, Father, for such was your gracious will. All things have been handed over to me by my Father, and no one knows the Son except the Father, and no one knows the Father except the Son and anyone to whom the Son chooses to reveal him. Come to me, all who labor and are heavy laden, and I will give you rest. Take my yoke upon you, and learn from me, for I am gentle and lowly in heart, and you will find rest for your souls. For my yoke is easy, and my burden is light.'"

What are your top three action steps?

1. _____

_____

2. _____

_____

3. _____

_____

What questions do you still have regarding the journey to an unhindered life? Brainstorm some people, places, or resources you can go to for further study and examination. What makes it difficult for us to lay our burdens down in exchange for Jesus' rest? What do we have to give up?

_____

_____

_____

_____

_____

_____

Write a short prayer asking for God's help in exchanging your burden for Christ's burden. Be honest about your struggles and ask for help in surrendering everything to Him.

_____

_____

_____

_____

_____

In your own words, define "emerging genius" as it's used in this chapter. What does this genius look like as it makes an appearance in your life?

_____

_____

_____

_____

_____

_____

How does your journey to an unhindered life benefit others?

_____

_____

_____

_____

_____

_____

_____

If you had to sum up what you've learned about yourself through this study in one sentence, what would it be?

_____

_____

_____

_____

_____

_____

Action Step: Who in your life might benefit from learning the lessons you've been learning so far? Are there any similarities in this person's heart story and your own? How can you reach out to this person and begin to build a supportive relationship? How can you encourage and edify them through what you've learned?

_____

_____

_____

_____

_____

_____

_____

_____

_____

_____

_____

_____

_____

_____

_____

_____

_____

_____

_____

_____

_____

_____

_____

_____

_____

_____

_____

_____

Writing Assignment: Each of us has a mission field. After completing this study, which people, or groups of people, is God calling you to reach out to and share His love with?

_____

_____

_____

_____

_____

_____

_____

_____

_____

_____

_____

_____

What's the Story of Your Heart?

This is a place to record your answers to some of the biggest questions, ideas, and reflection points in this study. Consider the chapters you've read, the notes you've taken, and the things God has revealed to you. Here's your opportunity to piece it all together and gain a clearer understanding of the story of your heart.

My Heart's Hindered Story:

_____

_____

_____

_____

_____

_____

_____

_____

_____

_____

_____

_____

_____

_____

My Sore Spot:

_____

_____

_____

_____

_____

_____

_____

_____

_____

_____

_____

_____

_____

_____

My Heart Logic (Life-Inspired):

_____

_____

_____

_____

_____

_____

_____

_____

_____

_____

_____

_____

_____

_____

_____

_____

_____

_____

_____

_____

_____

_____

_____

_____

_____

My Private Conclusions:

1) Little t truths:

_____

_____

_____

_____

_____

_____

_____

_____

_____

_____

2) Small s strategies:

_____

_____

_____

_____

_____

_____

_____

_____

_____

_____

_____

_____

_____

3) Life Lessons:

_____

_____

_____

_____

_____

_____

_____

_____

_____

_____

My Life Outcomes (Life-Inspired):

_____

_____

_____

_____

_____

_____

_____

_____

_____

_____

_____

_____

_____

My Heart's Unhindered Story:

_____

_____

_____

_____

_____

_____

_____

_____

_____

_____

_____

_____

_____

_____

_____

God's Alternative for my Sore Spot:

_____

_____

_____

_____

_____

_____

_____

_____

_____

_____

_____

_____

_____

_____

_____

_____

_____

_____

_____

_____

_____

_____

_____

_____

_____

My Heart Logic (God-Inspired):

_____

_____

_____

_____

_____

_____

_____

_____

_____

_____

_____

My Private Conclusions:

_____

_____

_____

_____

_____

_____

_____

_____

_____

_____

_____

_____

_____

Big T Truths:

_____

_____

_____

_____

_____

_____

_____

_____

_____

_____

_____

_____

Big S Strategies:

_____

_____

_____

_____

_____

_____

_____

_____

_____

_____

_____

_____

_____

God Lessons:

_____

_____

_____

_____

_____

_____

_____

_____

_____

_____

_____

_____

_____

_____

_____

_____

My Life Outcomes (God-Inspired):

_____

_____

_____

_____

_____

_____

_____

_____

_____

_____

_____

_____

_____

_____

_____

_____

_____

_____

_____

_____

_____

_____

_____

_____

_____

_____

_____

My Personalized Message:

_____

_____

_____

_____

_____

_____

_____

_____

_____

_____

_____

_____

CPSIA information can be obtained
at www.ICGtesting.com
Printed in the USA
LVHW080317150821
695353LV00013B/1066